DATE DUE 6/05

AUG 0 6 2005			

DEMCO 38-296

SPLASH!

Poems of Our Watery World

Constance Levy

illustrations by David Soman

Orchard Books New York

An Imprint of Scholastic Inc.

Library of Congress Cataloging-in-Publication Data
Levy, Constance. Splash! : poems of our watery world /
by Constance Levy ; illustrated by David Soman.
p. cm.
Summary: More than thirty poems celebrate water in its
myriad forms, from the ocean to a droplet of dew.
ISBN 0-439-29318-9 (alk. paper)
1. Water—Juvenile poetry. 2. Children's poetry, American.
[1. Water—Poetry. 2. American poetry.] I. Soman, David, ill. II. Title.
PS3562.E9256 S65 2002   811'.54–dc21   2001034004

10 9 8 7 6 5 4 3   04 05 06

Printed in the United States of America   37
First edition, April 2002
Text has been set in 13 point Garamond Book.
Book design by Mina Greenstein

To Noah, Jonah, Adina, and Evyn

—C.L.

For Lucia, born into water

—D.S.

Contents

SPLASH!

Poems of
Our Watery World

Drops

A teardrop
looks like sadness
and has a salty taste.
A raindrop tastes of sky
and brings a shower.

A dewdrop is a new drop,
a taste-of-morning-brew drop
and is probably delicious
to a flower.

Sailing

Ah, when the wind
is in the mood
to fill your sails
with rich sail food,
you hear their gulps
and lip-smacking snaps
as their bellies billow
and your jacket flaps!

You think: what push-power,
what an event,
with only salt air
for nourishment,

as the water parts
and the boat
and crew
and you

s a i l   t h r o u g h!

Rainbow Making

To make a rainbow,
light must learn to paint

with beads of water
mixed with air
just right,

and master every color
row by row
to shape a bow.

It seems to take
a lot of stormy tries
to watercolor-paint
on misty skies.

Splash!

See how the stream
suddenly leaps
loose and free
from the mountain's brink.
See how it flings
its silvery spray,
singing a rain song
along the way.
Feel how it lands
with bursts of power,
splashing a wonderful
waterfall shower!

Turtle Says

On land
I'm a mud soldier
in a homemade helmet,
slowpoking my way along.
I'm told
I creep
like a sleepwalker,
and it's true.
             No matter.
In water,
on the other hand,
I'm a star,
a swooper, a glider,
a leaper, a flyer,
a ballet dancer
in my green tutu.
That's true too.

"A Watched Pot Never Boils"

*T*he fire glows
and I grow hot,
the water says,

but I will boil much better
in the pot,
unwatched,

so
go away
and stir the sauce
or grate the cheese,
please,
till you hear my bubbly song
saying: *Ready for spaghetti!*

I won't be long. . . .

Clare's Butterfly

"My hand is not a flower,
yellow butterfly," said Clare,
as she stepped out of the swimming pool
to find him landing there

by a tiny, shiny droplet
he had spotted from the air.

"You are sitting on my knuckle,
not a petal; don't you care?"

No, he seemed to answer,
I'm as hungry as a bear.
And he dipped into the droplet
for a picnic lunch
on Clare.

Ocean Rhythms

Wave after wave,
each wave
a beat
each beat
repeating
each stretch
receding.
This is Earth's
old wild heart
beating.

Plink by Plink

In the black of this cave
where bats bunk by day
and spelunkers with lanterns
push darkness away,
water spots linger
with juice
from the rock,
then drop
plink
by plink
liquid ticks
liquid tocks.

The stalactites that hang
stiff and icicle-like,
the stalagmites that jut
from below
were formed in that way,
plink by plink
day by day
starting hundreds or more
years ago.

Flood Line

*T*he river overflowed its banks
and all that I could see
were bright green tops
of flooded trees
poking up
like broccoli.

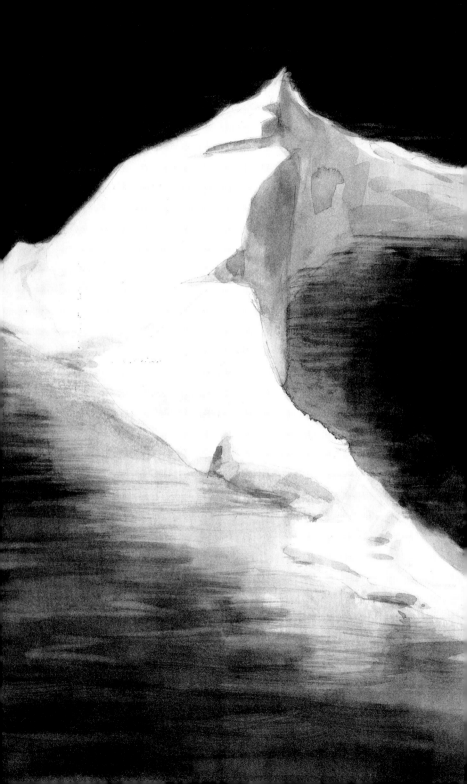

Iceberg

I am a glacier's child,
a beautiful mountain
of rock-hard snow.
Sailors fear me
and steer clear;
they say I'm dangerous
and wild.
They know

I'm hiding most of me
below the rolling sea.

You may find me here one day
where great whales play,
    doing what I do
    going where I go.
But remember what they say!

Waves I Meet

Some waves I meet
on sandy shores
are spit and anger
and they roar
and knock me off my feet
before
they snicker softly
and retreat.

And some waves
scamper
up the beach
the way a puppy runs to greet
someone it knows
to lick his toes.

Pour

Water,
pour a silver stream
slim and sparkling,
sharp of aim
into the glass
to an inch of the rim.
Soon I will spoon
white sugar
while you wait
and the juice
of a yellow lemon
as its mate,
to tease and tingle
the tongue,
then I will stir
until they mingle
with you
as one
and we have made
lemonade.

Yum!

Dragonfly

Dragonfly is sewing
summer stitches
in the silky pond
with her tail.

Up she goes and down
again
setting one small egg
with every stitch.

Darning is her duty
and she does it without fail,
to keep this pond, so rich with life,
adorned in dragon beauty.

Soap Bubbles

They could have named them
ghost jewels
or soap spheres
or rainbow moons,

water poppers,
froth bees—
names that might have stuck.

Imagine, "Let's blow water poppers,"
or "Ready for your froth bee bath?"

I think it's lucky
somebody,
somewhere,
took the trouble

to fit it all
in one good word
and named a bubble
BUBBLE!

Sea World

A creamy white
anemone
rocks
to the rhythm
of the sea.
A scallop yawns
and quickly closes.
A hidden pink-jawed lobster
dozes,
and jeweled fish
in fluid skies
flit here and there
like butterflies.

Water Dish

Hurry, cardinal
that brown sparrow is bathing
in your drinking water!

Fog

 love you,
fuzzy foggy air,
so dewy wet
and white

because without you
who would know
what walking in a cloud
is like?

In Dew Time

Run!
The juicy grass
will splash your feet;
the morning mist
will wash your sleepy face.

Discover how
bright bugs of sparkling dew
light up a spider's
lacy hiding place.

Don't wait.

The thirsty sun
is coming soon!

Teatime

*H*ow do you take your tea,
amber or gold
or Japanese green?
Tepid or wispy with steam?
Will you have cream?

One lump or two
to sweeten the brew?
A cookie, a crumpet, a scone?

How is your cat?
Do you think it will rain?
What an elegant hat!
Was it sunny in Spain?

May I pour you
some more?

Full Moon
on Mirror Lake

Tonight
on this still,
smooth lake
high
in its forest place,
the wandering,
wondering moon
becomes acquainted
with his face.

Laundry

Whether
by hands
kneading the cloth
in a flowing river
and scrubbing with rocks
the old-fashioned way,

or with the ease
of the swish and spin
of a washing machine,

it's water's work
(or is it play?)
to tease away
the grime
that we
put in.

Water Wizard

I am a wizard of shapes and moods:
I'm ice, I'm fog.
I grow your food.

I quench your thirst,
I flood, I launder,
I mirror, I skip,
I race, I wander.

I dribble and drip,
I float a ship.

I soothe a throat,
I brew your tea.

I swim in you,
you swim in me.

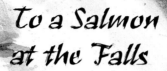

To a Salmon
at the Falls

*T*hrough foam
you leap,
a silver twist,
uncurling
as you fall.
You miss

and try again.

Up into
the swift down-rush
of water wild
and furious
you fling yourself,
more bird than fish,

to hang an instant in the air.

Again, you miss.

I stand here peering
through the mist
at water white
as winter snow,
watching you try.
I hope you know

I wish you luck
and quick success,
brave shining, silver
salmon fish.

Alligator Mother

*H*ow sly she is!
How sharp her teeth!
How strong, how quick
her snapping jaws
that draw her victims
underneath
the thick green swamp
that she calls home!

But now
she's just a mother,
cautious
as she takes
her pod of babies
piggyback
through water
rippling with snakes.

A Body of Water

If
what my teacher said
is true
(or was he joshing?)

that we are made
of mostly water
through and through,

don't you think
when I did cartwheels
after school

I would, at least,
have heard
a little *sloshing*?

Tasty Snowflakes

High-flying travelers,
you make my taste buds
hum.
You are winter
sky-pickles
to my warm-as-summer
tongue,
so cold
and so refreshing
that I relish
every one!

River Games

You're a river
full of fun
and mischief,
twirling
your whirlpools,
bobbing debris,
rushing past towns
full speed and free
then, WHAM!
A dam.

Bathwater Remembers

I have ridden with waves
that pounded the shores

and run in rivers
with sandpaper tongues,
scraping their beds,
when the world was young.

I have risen in mist
from the Indian Ocean,
rained on the Mediterranean Sea.
I have made wide lakes of hollow spaces.

I've been places!

Snap Beans

Do plants
feel thirst
as we do
when their
parched leaves
droop sadly?
Do their limp stems
ache for water
as they urge
tired roots
to seek
life-giving juice?

Is it true
that now,
after the rain,
this fresh green
fragrance
in the air
is from the sighs
of happy
snap beans?

Rain, Dance!

Rain,
you cloud head,
Wake up!

Stretch those mile-long legs
down here and dance.
Shuffle your nimble feet
over leaf tops.
Do the grass-tap;
do the petal-patter.
Make your drizzle sizzle!

We green things
are bored here,
way
deep
to
our
roots.

C'mon, let's celebrate.
Make Thunder
clap!

Thirst

*H*ave you ever felt
a dryness,
tongue to tooth,
and a nagging throat
that begged for water?

I have too!

That's why I understand
the daring squirrel
who plucked a ripe tomato
from my vine

and boldly sits
and sips
the stolen juice.

Barges

A caravan
pushed by a tow
long as a football field,
watch it go

heading up the Mississippi,
steady and slow.

Wonder what it's carrying—
steel, grain, sand?
Hundreds of tons, I'd guess,

but the river will hold it
like a baby in its hand
as it strolls and races and
meanders
through the land.

Who needs a movie or a TV show
when you've got a river
with a barge and tow!

Skipping Pebbles

*F*ind a shore
and pick a pebble,
a flat one
you can spin.
Do not plunk it
or slam dunk it;
fling it sidewise
just to skim
the water skin.

Make it touch
as dragonflies do,
skip
and touch
and skip again,
to raise a row
of water rings
that grow and grow
and then—

pick a pebble.
Fling it in. . . .